Elephants in the Church

CONVERSATIONS WE CAN'T AFFORD TO IGNORE

BEACON HILL PRESS
OF KANSAS CITY

Elephants in the Church

CONVERSATIONS WE CAN'T AFFORD TO IGNORE

Editor
Mike L. Wonch
Assistant Editor
Duane Brush
Amanda Neufeld
Director of Curriculum
Merritt J. Nielson

ISBN: 978-0-8341-2979-5
Printed in U.S.A.

10 9 8 7 6 5 4 3 2 1

CONTENTS

Are there certain topics that you don't feel comfortable discussing everywhere . . . or anywhere? Each of us has things we would rather not talk about in certain social circles or with a particular group of people. Why? Maybe we feel some things are better left unsaid. Maybe we feel some subjects shouldn't be shared in mixed company, or at work, or at home, or wherever. Some topics we may feel are appropriate to discuss in some places, but not in other places. For instance, we do not hesitate talking about our political views with close friends but may feel reluctant to share these same views during an office staff meeting. There may be certain topics we choose to overlook simply because we do not feel comfortable talking about them, especially in church.

Elephants in the Church tackles the issues that we choose to ignore within the body of Christ. On the pages of this book the authors will talk about those topics that need to be talked about rather than avoided. The intention is not to create conflict between people of differing opinions, but to bring subjects to the surface that we have chosen not to face head on. Issues such as:

- *How do we create an open atmosphere for conversation within the church?*
- *Is there anything wrong with having material possessions?*
- *Does prejudice exist in the church?*
- *What is the Christian view of sexual sin?*
- *How do we help victims of abuse?*
- *Do Christians have acceptable addictions?*
- *Does God favor one political party over another?*

Each chapter tackles these questions in a way that allows the reader to begin to think through the topics critically, but more importantly, biblically.

Dr. David Holdren has served as pastor, principle, and General Superintendent in the Wesleyan Church. He holds a B.A. in Religion from Owosso College, a Master of Divinity from Asbury Theological Seminary, a Master Degree in Education from Ball State, and an Honorary Doctorate from Indiana Wesleyan University and Houghton College. He and his wife Marlene have been married for 46 years, have two daughters and six grandchildren. He and his wife currently reside in Maria, Ohio.

Eric Forgrave lives in Grandview, MO with his beautiful wife Beth and three children. He is pastor of Grandview Church of the Nazarene and has been part of this church in some capacity since 1998 (seminary student, youth pastor, pastor).

Kevin Hancock serves as senior pastor at the Good Samaritan Church of the Nazarene in Collinsville, IL. He has served as Pastor to Youth and Families at churches in Springfield (IL), Detroit, and Kansas City. He is a graduate from Olivet Nazarene University and Nazarene Theological Seminary. Kevin and his wife, Sarah, have two boys, Braxton and Trenton.

Mike Wonch serves as Senior Editor for WordAction Publishing Company. Mike is a graduate of MidAmerica Nazarene University and Nazarene Theological Seminary. He and his wife Jeremi have been married for 25 years. Their son Seth is a junior at Olivet Nazarene University. Mike and his family reside in Olathe, Kansas.

Mark Littleton is a freelance writer who resides in Gladstone, Missouri.

Willie Rice graduated from MidAmerica Nazarene University in 2006 with a Bachelor's degree in Bible and Theology. While attending Nazarene Theological Seminary he worked in the Archives department at the International Headquarters of the Church of the Nazarene. Willie lives in Topeka, KS with his wife Whitney, also a MidAmerica graduate, and their two children Hughes and Vaughn.

Dr. Jon Jonston is professor of sociology at Pepperdine University in Malibu, California.

Creating An Open Atmosphere for Conversations

Hospitality

I am normally the first to arrive at my church each Sunday morning. As I unlock the building, I've made it a conscious habit to pray for those who may be walking through the doors. I pray that as they enter they would encounter the loving presence of God among His people as we worship, learn and fellowship together. I pray that God would make His people into a holy people who authentically welcome others with arms (and lives) wide open.

We understand that God calls us to build godly relationships with others. But how do we unlock the doors of fellowship, creating a genuine environment of openness to others? How do we become a church where "outsiders" are genuinely welcomed to become "insiders," sincerely accepted into congregational life and ministry? How do we create an atmosphere for spiritual conversations within the church? Certainly it's the work of the Spirit in establishing unity in love among us. Yet we still play a crucial role in allowing God to establish us into a holy people, marked by Christ's love and a concern for openness to others outside and inside the church.

Hospitality played a crucial role in the mission of the early church. Acts chapter 2 provides a window through which we see the early church's effectiveness in becoming an authentic community of acceptance and love. Luke paints the picture of a "missional" church who served as an open door to others.

> "All the believers were together and had everything in common. Selling their possessions and goods, they gave to anyone as he had need. Everyday they continued to meet together in the temple courts. They broke bread in their homes and ate together with glad and sincere hearts, praising God and enjoying the favor of all the people" (Acts 2:44-47*a*).

It was a contagious kind of fellowship. Outsiders were drawn within by their love. Nothing was hidden. All was shared. We're told the effect this kind of Spirit-filled hospitality had on people: *"the Lord added to their number daily those who were being saved"* (Acts 2:47). The apostle Paul was clear and concise in his instructions to the Christians in ancient Rome. *"Practice hospitality"* he told them (Rom. 12:13). It was a vital key to unlocking the door to genuine fellowship with one another.

The Greek word for *"practice"* literally means to *"pursue."* It speaks of an intensity of effort in earnest pursuit of another, as in chasing down a criminal. Paul uses the term in a positive sense to reinforce the energy and intensity with which Christians are called to welcome outsiders. The Greek word translated *"hospitality"* implies offering friendship to strangers. Paul's instruction to the church to practice hospitality was a call to be ministers of God's reconciliation to a world estranged from Him. It was a call to pursue those who weren't already intimately connected within the circle of fellowship, for the purpose of demonstrating the loving friendship offered by God.

Reflect on this...

How would you define hospitality?

Who are the people that we may consider "strangers"?

From Acts 2:44-47, what were the characteristics of the early church?

In ancient eastern culture hospitality was as much a gift of necessity as anything else. It was long before the days of *Holiday Inn*. Those required to travel beyond their own community needed shelter. Offering weary travelers shelter in their time of need was more than a gift; it was a highly-valued expectation. While hospitality should never come at the price of anyone's safety, it's certainly clear from the Scriptures that Christian hospitality is critical to a church marked by loving acceptance and openness.

The contemporary church has in some ways lost sight of the true value of hospitality. We are extremely disconnected from one another. We don't really know each other. We may desire a sense of authenticity in our relationships, but we're too busy running our kids to and from soccer practice to create the time and space needed to truly know and be known by each other. And who needs to invite people we barely know into our homes when there's plenty of rooms at the *Motel 6*? Besides, getting the house cleaned up for guests takes a lot of work. Right?

Reflect on this...

In what ways do you see hospitality practiced in the church?

In what ways do you see hospitality lacking in the church?

Read Romans 12:9-13 and reflect on how these verses relate to the Church.

I'm convinced that two of Satan's most useful contemporary tools are the vacuum cleaner and the garage door opener. They keep Christians from offering God's gift of hospitality and the deep and meaningful relationships that often emerge. The vacuum cleaner and garage door opener both serve as easy excuses for keeping the doors of intimate fellowship locked tight.

One of the excuses often cited for not inviting others into our homes is that the house is too messy. We don't want anyone to see the stacks of papers that pile up on the kitchen table, or the dirty dishes in the sink, or the dirty socks in the hallway. Heaven forbid anyone might think our home doesn't always look like a photo out of Better Homes and Gardens. We worry incessantly what guests might think if our house isn't completely spotless. The vacuum cleaner becomes an excuse for not going the extra mile to invite neighbors inside, to see us as we truly live, dirty socks and all.

The garage door opener also aids in fostering shallow relationships. The clicker has made it incredibly easy to never leave the comfort and safety of our own home. We don't have to go outside. We need not be inconvenienced by encountering our neighbors face-to-face. We need not learn their names, let alone sacrifice the time and energy necessary to build a meaningful relationship. No messy spiritual conversations required. We can just smile and wave as we pass by from the comfort of our vehicle. The incessant demand for convenience often comes at the price of genuine friendship.

Building meaningful and intimate relationships requires time, energy, and sacrifice. There are significant risks we take when we invite strangers into our lives. Openness and vulnerability can leave us wounded. If we unlock the doors of our soul some might take advantage of us. Letting those who have a different viewpoint engage us in conversation may challenge what we believe. Engaging others in love is hard work. Of course, the gift of hospitality implies something much greater than just allowing someone to physically enter our home. At the heart of hospitality is a willingness to allow others into our lives. To see us as we truly live. To know us and to be known by us. When we refuse to welcome others to see us as we truly are is to deny them the opportunity to share with us the grace that God extends to them.

An atmosphere of openness takes root as we release our incessant need to display a life that's always tidy, refusing others the chance to see God's wisdom and power at work in our confusion and weakness. While the Scriptures tell us that God desires our hearts be cleansed from sin, we must guard against thinking that we can come to a place where we no longer need to confess our sins to God or others. The fact is we are a work in progress. We all unintentionally misunderstand, disappoint, or even hurt others. One key to unlocking openness is to admit that, just like everyone else, God is still working on us.

Building meaningful, intimate relationships requires time, energy, and sacrifice.

We must be willing to allow others to see that God is transforming us. That kind of transparency is inviting to others (who also don't have their lives all squeaky clean). And in a culture that fosters and encourages lying, that kind of honesty can become part of the transforming work God seeks in all our lives—insider and outsider alike.

Ultimately, a church that is characterized by genuine openness is one in which each member is obediently following our loving Savior. We cannot replicate the genuine love of Christ for the stranger in our midst apart from each member of the body surrendering fully to the work of the Spirit. Only as we allow Christ to dwell in us will we receive that same kind of passionate love for others that Paul stirs up within the Church in Rome when he calls them to practice hospitality.

If you desire to be a church marked by openness, then go unlock the doors. Invite neighbors into your home. Give them an open door into your lives. Take the time to get acquainted. Enter into conversations that lead to a deeper walk with Christ., Let them see you for who you truly are, daily needing and benefiting from the cleansing and sanctifying work of God through Christ.

Reflect on this...

What are the barriers to building meaningful relationships?

What are the ways you can begin to create an atmosphere of genuine openness to others?

NOTES:

2

When Is Enough Enough?

Materialism

Solomon should have been one of the most materialistic people of all time. He had so much wealth he ignored his silver and measured his riches only in gold. If ever anyone knew the satisfactions of wealth, it was Solomon. Yet, many Bible scholars believe Solomon was the unidentified writer of Ecclesiastes, that woeful pessimist who bemoaned, among other things, the worthlessness of wealth. "Whoever loves money never has money enough," the writer lamented; "whoever loves wealth is never satisfied with his income" (Ecclesiastes 5:10). The fact is most people never know when enough is enough. This is the main problem with materialism.

In our society, many seem to be afraid of living within their means. We feel the pull to keep accumulating "stuff" in an effort to show that we are not poor and to gain the respect of those around us. Many find refuge in the suburbs where the homeless, hungry, and poverty-stricken are camouflaged, if not completely hidden. We often avoid any place where the broken and bleeding edge of human sorrow can be seen.

People who are poor-by-choice seem to be a problem for many in our society. These individuals challenge some of our fundamental assumptions about life—the importance of succeeding financially. Many see financial success as an important achievement and something to be valued. (That is, if the accumulation of unneeded and overpriced "things" is to be considered an achievement.)

Reflect on this...

Read Ecclesiastes 5:10. Do you think people are ever satisfied with the amount of money they have? Why, or why not?

How far would you be willing to take the "poor-by-choice" mentality? Explain.

People have struggled with the poor-by-choice for hundreds of years. In 1182, Giovanni Francesco Bernadone was born to a wealthy Italian cloth merchant in Assisi. In his early 20s, disillusioned by materialism, he renounced his inherited wealth and gave his possessions to the poor. He left home dressed in a ragged cloak and a rope belt from a scarecrow. His father legally disinherited him, and his church didn't know what to do with him. Though he (known to us today as Francis of Assisi) did not aggressively seek converts to his simpler way of life, many people chose to follow his example. Soon a new order, the Franciscans, was approved by the Catholic Church.

The Jewish culture into which Jesus was born was, in some ways, not much different from today. They didn't know what to do with the poor-by-choice either. In fact, they had rules against it. The rabbis of Jesus' day taught that you were not to give away more than 20 percent of your wealth, for fear you might become a burden on society. In a commentary on Deuteronomy 28:15-58, one rabbi wrote, "No portion in life is harder to bear than poverty, for he who is crushed by poverty is as one beset by all the afflictions in the world, indeed, as one stricken by the curses listed in Deuteronomy."[1]

Reflect on this...

Francis of Assisi said, "For it is in giving that we receive." What do you think Francis meant by this statement?

Think back on your life. Has there ever been a time when serving Christ cost you something?

What do you think about being "poor by choice"? Is everyone called to this lifestyle?

The Rich Young Ruler

In Jesus' time, wealth was considered a sign of God's favor, and so rabbis were expected to be financially secure. They didn't have to be wealthy but needed to be at least moderately well-to-do to have the respect of the community. Yet, Jesus wasn't. He was a homeless, wandering preacher, with no dependable income. But something about Him generated great respect. One day, an important man came running after Jesus as He was leaving town. Having stopped Jesus, he knelt before Him. Matthew, Mark, and Luke all identified the one who knelt as a very rich man. Matthew recorded that he was young (19:20), and Luke added that he was a ruler (18:18). So we call him "the rich young ruler." This man had everything our culture values: youth, riches, prestige, and power in the community—a combination most people in every generation would love to have. Yet with it all, he knelt before Jesus.

The man asked the question, "What good thing *must* I do to get eternal life?" (Matthew 19:16, emphasis added). Jesus responded, "Keep the commandments." The man replied, "All these things I have kept since I was a young man" (v. 20). He had tried his best to be good and to keep all the commandments since his childhood. We may safely conclude that Jesus knew that the young man kneeling before Him was honestly seeking truth, a devout man who sincerely wanted to follow Him. Yet, He pressed on to the one thing the young man still needed. Jesus said to the rich young ruler, "Go, sell everything you have and give to the poor, and you will have treasure in heaven. Then come, follow me" (v. 21). When the rich young man asked Jesus what he needed to do in order to inherit eternal life, he was thinking in terms of what he could do to earn his way to heaven and to righteousness. At the same time, Jesus tried to tell him that a right relationship with God is a gift to be received—something God does within the hearts of those who follow.

"At this the man's face fell. He went away sad, because he had great wealth" (v. 22). He was sad and walked away. For him, the price of following Jesus was too high.

Reflect on this...

Why do you think the young man left rather than choosing to follow Jesus?

Think about a time when God asked you to do something you thought impossible. How did it impact your life?

The Disciples' Question

The rich young ruler chooses not to follow Jesus and leaves? The disciples asked a loaded question, "Who then can be saved" (v. 25)? Far more than lost status, their inquiry reveals their concern about their own future. Peter expressed the heartbeat of the group when he said, "We have left everything to follow you!" (v. 27) We know how to translate this concern: *If the man who had everything couldn't make it, what's going to happen to us? And don't forget, Lord, we've given up all we have to follow You.*

When the rich young ruler left, Jesus talked about a camel and the eye of a needle (Mark 10:24-25). Could a camel go through the eye of this needle? There appears to be more to Jesus' words than this example demonstrates. Jesus may have been thinking about a camel and an actual eye of a tailor's needle. Now that is sheer impossibility. And that is exactly Jesus' point. Jesus' words run counter to the human spirit, which thinks surely there is something we can do to earn our salvation. Yet, Jesus said, "Apart from me you can do nothing" (John 15:5). Concerning the salvation of all of us, not just the rich man, Jesus said to the disciples, "With man this is impossible, but not with God; all things are possible with God" (Mark 10:27). No one can inherit eternal life because of anything they own or do. In the camel story, the hyperbole emphasizes the impossibility.

In our humanness, we are tempted to limit this hard word from Jesus to the very rich. Francis of Assisi responded to the challenge of this passage by renouncing his family's wealth. The New Testament as a whole, however, does not require this of everyone. Wealthy people such as Lydia (Acts 16:14), Phoebe (Romans 16:1-2), Priscilla and Aquila (Romans 16:3-5), and Gaius (Romans 16:23) played important roles in the spread of the gospel by making their spacious homes available for Christian gatherings. More significant than the renunciation of wealth itself, Mark's story teaches the renunciation of the attitudes characteristic of the world of the wealthy. Ultimately, if we listen to God's Word, we'll see that, while the demands of discipleship will vary from individual to individual, discipleship takes on the form of the cross for every believer.

Nothing less than a willingness to give everything to Jesus will ever meet the Master's demands. The joyous truth, however, in regard to our salvation is that "what is impossible with men is possible with God" (Luke 18:27). So the question for all of us becomes a matter of where we put our trust—in what we have and can do in Jesus. Consider the quote by martyred missionary Jim Elliot, "He is no fool who gives up what he cannot keep to gain what he cannot lose."

Nothing less than a willingness to give everything to Jesus will ever meet the Master's demands.

Reflect on this...

Jim Elliot said, "He is no fool who gives up what he cannot keep to gain what he cannot lose." What do you think he meant by this statement?

This week, take time to think about what it means to count the cost of following Christ.

NOTES:

3

Weighing Facts with Our Thumb on the Scales

Prejudice

On a recent trip to Bath, in England, I visited an opulent mansion once owned by William Beckford, an affluent resident of John Wesley's time. Oddly, there were stairs in the center of the living room, covered by a small roof. Our guide explained: *"The owner installed the roof so that it would be impossible for any 'lowly' servant to ever gaze down upon him from above. He must always be the one to look down on such persons."*[1]

Today such roofs aren't used to make people feel inferior. Instead, folks prefer to flaunt lavish jewelry and flashy cars, continuously namedrop or spit out big words, brag on themselves, ignore or insult others. Many will do most anything to feel superior and feed an insatiable appetite for pride.

Examining the Culprit

- *Pride and prejudice are closely linked.* According to the well-known theologian Paul Tillich, three kinds of vanity are the most likely facilitators of prejudice: **Pride of place** (residence or rung on class ladder), **Pride of face** (skin color or physical beauty), and **Pride of grace** (exclusion of all differing in belief or conviction).
- *Prejudice is sandwiched between two stages.* Stage 1 is the root of prejudice and Stage 3 is the fruit of prejudice.
  Stage 1: STEREOTYPING—making a mental judgment that the *other* is different, based on collective rather than individual grounds.
  Stage 2: PREJUDICE—negatively approaching the *different one* emotionally and attitudinally based on unreasonable or irrational stereotypes rather than individual merit.
  Stage 3: DISCRIMINATION—taking action to separate from the *different one.*

- *Prejudice is universal.* It thrives in all cultures. When cultures become so prejudicial that they are obsessed with their own uniqueness, they're said to be *ethnocentric.* In short, they see themselves as the only true measuring stick, and predictably, everyone else comes up short. Unfortunately, ethnocentrism is faithfully passed down to succeeding generations.

Thankfully, some victims of prejudice are becoming more vigorously defended. Though by no means totally obliterated, racism, sexism, and many limitations placed on the physically challenged appear to be receding. Nevertheless, sociologists contend that it remains "open season" for others. (For instance, those advanced in age, the obese, and even born-again believers.)

Reflect on this...

How do you respond to people who try to make themselves superior to others? What do you think is the true motivation of their actions?

What do you think causes people to be prejudiced? Do you think it is easy to change this kind of attitude and behavior?

Relentless Intruder

So far we've painted with a very broad brush. Our words have described people-at-large, many of whom have not experienced (nor applied) our Lord's transforming love.

What about the redeemed community of believers, the Church for whom Jesus died? Does prejudice rear its ugly head within its ranks? And if so, what forms does it take, how much damage does it wreak, and what can be done to purge it? Even in the Church, we ostracize many who seem dissimilar to ourselves. We have an affinity for folks like ourselves, but an aversion toward outsiders. We're especially prejudicial toward those we judge to be at fault for their own "unfortunate" plight, such as the poor, drug addicts, the divorced, alcoholics, and non-Christians. We may also add to this list "fallen" ministers or laypersons, dropouts, the homeless, victims of disease (e.g., AIDS), homosexuals, welfare recipients, ex-convicts, and persons who have tattoos and piercings.

Again, all of these have this in common: they are seen to be significantly different from "regular" people, and that difference is deemed to make them inferior. As a result, they are suspected of being untrustworthy, freeloaders, and even dangerous to intimately interact with.

To reach out to such isolated (distant) or insulated (different) persons—as Jesus did—is felt to be risky, costly, and fruitless. It can ultimately produce compassion fatigue and invite frustration.

The Incalculable Toll

Down deep we know (or should know) that our rejection of such persons hurts them deeply and prohibits us from being the light, salt, and leaven for the world that our Maker wishes us to be. Even more tragic, it contradicts everything we say we stand for—namely, being godly in character. Let's examine a couple of key components of God's character.

First, our loving, compassionate heavenly Father responds to all of us with **generous grace.** His arms of welcome and forgiveness remain always outstretched, as vividly portrayed in Jesus' parable of the prodigal son.

Second, His ultimate judgment of our lives, in the final essence, will be totally **impartial.** His Word declares that He is "a Father who judges each [person's] work impartially" (1 Peter 1:17).

Gracious and impartial. This strongly implies that pedigree, riches, power, status, or any other achievements or entitlements make no difference with Him. Each is judged on the basis of his or her own merits. Concerning pedigree in particular, as one declared: "God has no grandchildren, only children."

So, to follow His pattern will necessitate reflecting these wonderful qualities. In a word, we must be the very opposite of prejudiced.

Reflect on this...

Do think prejudice exists within the church? Why, or why not?

What are the ways you can help destroy prejudice and embrace the biblical mandate of love?

Purging the Enemy

Knowing the problem is necessary but not conclusive. To stop at knowing only provides remorse, a defensive spirit, or outright frustration. We must zero in on the solution. In short, how might prejudice be dispelled in our midst? How might we "defang," and ultimately destroy, this monster and embrace the biblical mandate of love? Though not exhaustive, it is hoped that these few suggestions may help.

First, we can minimize differences between ourselves and others by intentionally interfacing with them "on level ground."

As we spend time and exert energy interacting with people, an appreciation for them (and even their differences) usually forms. Result: the "strange" begins seeming less so, and inevitably, estrangement lessens or vanishes. In short, our perception changes as we no longer see others as a category. This is likely to dispel or radically reduce our level of prejudice over time.

Second, we must truly suspend punitive judgment. We must cut people some slack, realizing that we never comprehend the total, complex picture. Motives count, and we are not always able to ascertain them in others. Only God sees the heart and thus is the only One qualified to judge.

Only God sees the heart and thus is the only One qualified to judge.

In reality, our Lord loves us all equally, "not wanting anyone to perish, but everyone to come to repentance" (2 Peter 3:9). That goes for people who seem marginal, mistaken, and even mean—this world's perceived outcasts and losers.

Third, cultivate God-given sensitivities when interacting with or speaking of people who are different.

Going beyond the current rage of political correctness—which is often superficially staged for self-serving purposes—we must be careful of words and actions that hurt others. Why? Such persons already feel disadvantaged and hypersensitive. And in their shoes, we'd probably feel the same!

Fourth, get over the "accept the sinner = accepting the sin" mentality. We are sometimes tempted to think that by allowing certain people to attend our church or by reaching out to people whose lifestyles are contrary to Christianity we are in some way condoning or validating their beliefs and actions. We must get over this mentality and be the hands and feet of Christ to them. We can reach out to others without compromising our faith or the message of God's Word.

Who Deserves a Roof?

In Bath, William Beckford's roof symbolized his arrogance and flaming prejudice. Just the thought of ever being looked down upon by any lowly servant seemed revolting. His roof was intended to prevent that.

Employing the same metaphor, we should construct roofs for this world's weak, lowly, and disenfranchised. They deserve to *never* be looked down upon with disdain, but instead should be seen as valued equals—as persons whom God loved sufficiently to send His only Son for their salvation.

Above everyone, we as Christians have the least reason to look down on anyone. Why? Our only value is based on God's love for us, not any earned or confirmed bestowment we have attained. Furthermore, the best possible way we serve Him is by becoming true servants to His most needy children.

In actuality, we have much in common with targets of prejudice. The Bible declares us to be mere aliens (transients) in a strange land. Peter admonishes us to "live [our] lives as strangers here in reverent fear" (1 Peter 1:17). While doing so, we're promised lives of rejection. Paul doesn't mince words: "Everyone who wants to live a godly life in Christ Jesus will be persecuted" (2 Timothy 3:12).

Our very rejection gives us great reason to identify with, and tightly embrace, all who are rejected. And in so doing, we have the greatest potential for offering such persons true empathy, comfort, and hope.

With this in mind, it is clear why our Lord primarily concentrated His loving attention on the lowly—defending, healing, forgiving, and empowering. And their response was overwhelming. Likewise, as a matter of record, targets of abuse have consistently been the most responsive to the gospel throughout history.

Our mandate is crystal clear: *Following our Lord's wise and compassionate example, we must befriend and offer reconciling dignity to all who are declared "unworthy" by our world.* Indeed, this is our high calling.

Reflect on this...

The author says, "Following our Lord's wise and compassionate example, we must befriend and offer reconciling dignity to all who are declared 'unworthy' by our world." How well do you feel you are doing at following the "Lord's wise and compassionate example?"

Pray this week, asking God to make you aware of any prejudiced actions or attitudes you might have toward others.

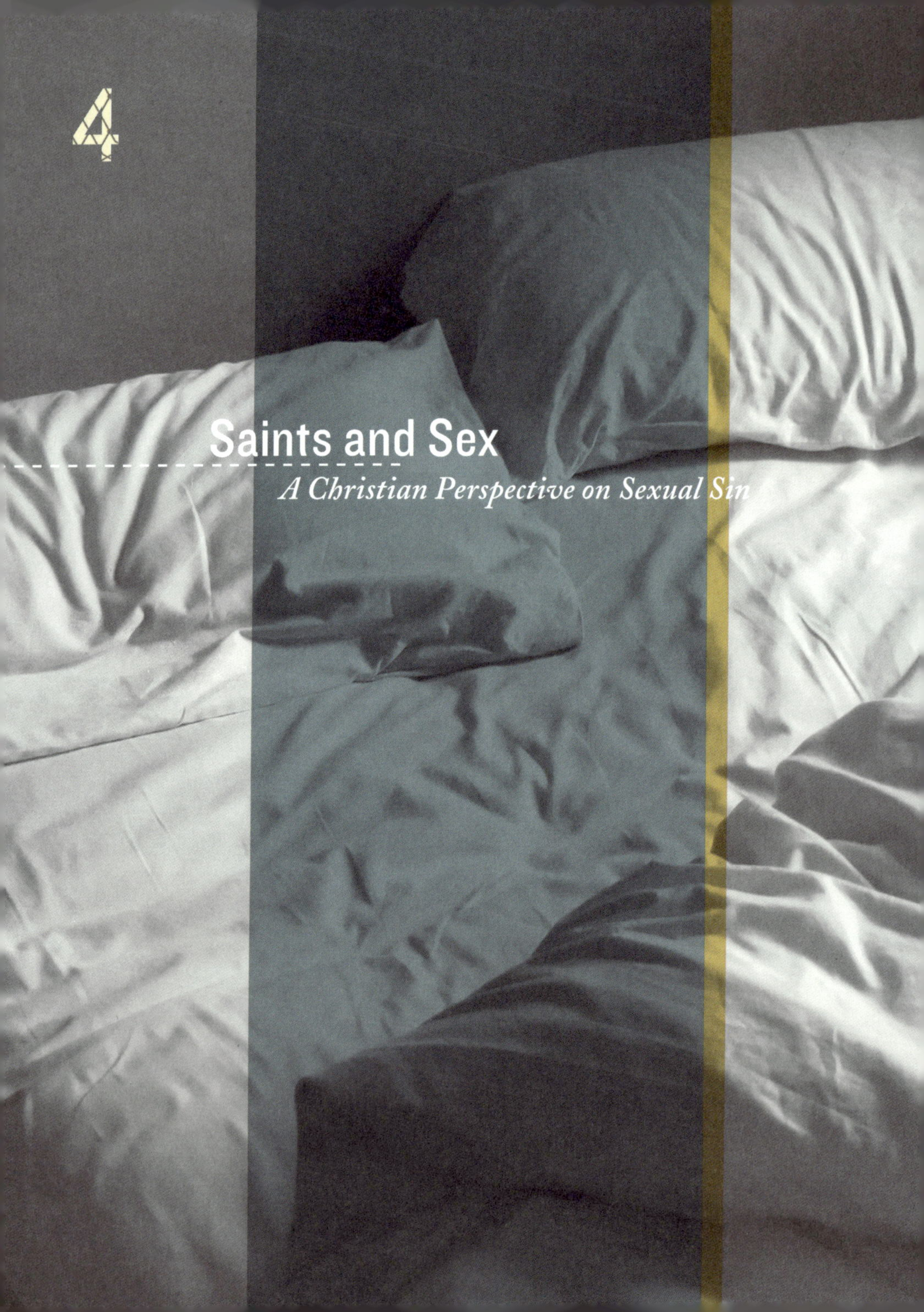

4

Saints and Sex

A Christian Perspective on Sexual Sin

I am going to begin this chapter with four statements that may kindle your wrath toward me. First, many forms of sexual promiscuity (sin) are understandable. *I did not say excusable or acceptable, but understandable.* If a person did not possess moral values and prohibitions and significant self-discipline regarding sexual activity, then it would be understandable why he or she might pursue it. Take away the guidelines and guardrails, and sexual fulfillment is, for many, one of life's most important goals.

Second, it seems that the capacity for sex is one of the aspects of our nature that God created. The two main purposes for our sexual capacities are procreation and pleasure.

Third, Christians seem about as vulnerable to sexual sinning as anyone else. I firmly believe there are many, many Christians who have steadfastly resisted powerful and persistent temptations and remained true to Christ and their loved ones. Maybe a better way of saying what I mean is that the number of Christians who do yield to sexual temptations, fully aware of the potential consequences, seems confusing and disappointing.

Finally, there is a kind of hypocrisy existing across Christendom that may increase our overall vulnerability to failure in these areas—it is easy to focus our attention on certain sins while ignoring others. For example, we are really tough on homosexuality, as though "regular" sexual sins do not count as much against us. We exhibit the same tendency when we focus on the unacceptability of using alcohol or tobacco but are much more tolerant toward gluttony, gossip, mean-spiritedness, and dysfunctional family relationships.

Source of Sexual Sin

If we are really serious about avoiding sexual sin, we need to look for its source in our lives. First of all, we should strike God off the list. God did create the capacity, but does not use it against us. James 1:13 says, "When tempted, no one should say, 'God is tempting me.'"

God created us as sexual beings. In light of this, these same urges that promote healthy, legitimate sexual expression also open us up to temptation to commit sexual sins. For example, our inclination to experience pleasure is natural, but can also be used in a way that goes against God's commands. Another example is our desire and attraction for the opposite sex. It is right and natural for two single people to meet, be attracted to one another, and fall in love. However, this same desire and attraction can be sinfully distorted if it occurs between two married people (not to each other) who allow attraction and desire to lead to sin.

Other sources and less innocent motivations can be the exercise of power, punishment, and control. These also might include things as simple and common as peer pressure, cultural endorsement, and even unexpected opportunity. Not to be overlooked is that personal force of evil, the devil, whose mission seems to be to corrupt every good thing God has made to bring about ungodly consequences.

God gives us deliverance from above sources. However, in order to provide the best resistance against temptation and sin, we must do something as well.

Reflect on this...

Do we, in the Church, have a tendency to treat and view some sexual sins as being different from others? If so, how?

How do we challenge their lifestyle in a way that could draw them to openness before the Holy Spirit, who will lead them in the truth?

Saints and Sex

One of the passages in the Bible I have heard preached on many times was a verse that highlights holiness. 1 Thessalonians 4:3-4 says, "It is God's will that you should be sanctified [holy]." The pastors I heard quote this verse rarely continued the sentence, which says, "that you should avoid sexual immorality; that each of you should learn to control your own body in a way that is holy and honorable."

Amazingly, this verse indicates to us that a major feature of holiness is *body control!* The same concept is shouted out in the more commonly used verse from Romans 12:1, "I urge you, brothers and sisters, in view of God's mercy, to offer *your bodies* as living sacrifices, holy and pleasing to God" (emphasis added).

Sainthood and sex are intimately connected in Scripture. Why do sexual sins seem to rank so high on the taboo scale? Are sexual sins more evil than non-sexual sins? Is it because of their pervasiveness? Are these the most common sins among us?

Sexual sins deserve the attention they get *not* because sex is a bad thing. It was actually created holy and right for humankind. They deserve attention because this kind of sin has a way of destroying relationships and the integrity of an individual soul. It violates trust and honor and shreds the dignity of a human being. Sexual sins can lead people to be "separated from the life of God . . . due to the hardening of their hearts. Having lost all sensitivity, they have given themselves over to sensuality so as to indulge in every kind of impurity, and they are full of greed" (Ephesians 4:18-19).

Reflect on this...

How do you deal with a temptation to act upon a desire you know is contrary to God's will?

Why is it important for people to understand the difference between temptation and sin?

Temptation itself is not sin

Temptation and Crossing the Line

Temptation itself is not sin, but if pandered to, "it gives birth to sin" (James 1:15). We cannot always prevent a tempting scene or thought from crossing our path, but we can organize our life and lifestyle to reduce our exposure to temptation. Each person will need to figure out how to do that in his or her environment. What we do with the temptation determines whether it becomes sin. It is like anger in the sense that to experience feelings of anger is not always wrong. What we do with those feelings determines whether it becomes sin (Ephesians 4:26). Temptation becomes sin when we give in to it. Having said that, here are a few thoughts that might help you avoid the pitfalls of sexual temptation and sin:

- Avoid listening and viewing things that lead to temptation. Steer clear of television shows, magazines, music, and so on that lead your mind to impure sexual thoughts and feelings.
- Avoid situations and actions that could lead to inappropriate behavior. Are your actions and reactions to another person Christlike? Do the things you say and do with a coworker, fellow church member, or friend cross the line of godly character?
- Surrender your thought life to Christ. We cannot control every thought that comes in to our minds, but we do control what we do with those thoughts.
- Build in safeguards. Safeguards build parameters that help you avoid things that could lead to sinful actions.
- Read God's Word. The Bible gives guidance for avoiding sexual immorality. Keeping our minds pure, talking appropriately, and thinking about godly things are things that the Bible says are important for keeping on the right track. Keeping God's Word in our hearts and minds will help avoid the dangers of sexual sin.
- Listen to the Holy Spirit. At some point, people who sin have decided to ignore God's leading Spirit and do their own thing. If something feels wrong, it very well may be God's presence telling you to stop.
- Don't think it couldn't happen to you. Although we should not live in paranoia, we should never think that we are not susceptible to sin. Take the words of Peter to heart: "Be alert and of sober mind. Your enemy the devil prowls around like a roaring lion looking for someone to devour" (1 Peter 5:8).

As Christians, we have to apply Paul's advice to *flee* temptation, *fight* the devil's attempts to trap us, and *follow* after righteousness.

Faithful

We often identify faithfulness, in a marriage for example, with what we did **not** do. However, being faithful includes what we **do** to bless, build, and sanctify a relationship. Faithfulness is getting really good at doing what love does (1 Corinthians 13:4-8; Galatians 5:22-23; Romans 12:9-21). Please read those passages carefully and repeatedly and ask the Holy Spirit to help you put them into practice. Then, watch every important relationship in your life soar and take on new meaning. Don't wait for other people to do their part first. You initiate and sustain what is good to do.

Reflect on this...

Think about a time when you used the "flee, fight, and follow" formula. How did it help you avoid giving into temptation?

Think about the word "faithful" and how it applies to keeping your thoughts and actions sexually pure.

Read 1 Corinthians 13:4-8; Galatians 5:22-23; Romans 12:9-21. Ask the Holy Spirit to help you put them into practice this week.

NOTES:

5

Behind Closed Doors

Abuse

Hearing the Voiceless

Twelve seconds. Not a significant amount of time to do much of anything: blow your nose, put in a stick of gum, set the alarm, or open the garage door. But in the time it takes you to count to 12—another act of domestic violence will occur; another case of child abuse will be reported; another elderly person will be neglected; and countless other sufferers of abuse will remain voiceless and isolated by their abusers.[1]

The National Center on Elder Abuse estimates that between 1 and 2 million Americans age 65 or older have been injured, exploited, or mistreated by someone they the depended on for care or protection. Every day, five children die as a result of abuse in the United States. Over 1,100 women are murdered each year by an intimate partner (average of three each day).[2] Close to a million women are abused each year (and report it), and over a million women are stalked by their intimate partners.[3] These are just a few of the many statistics I could share with you about abuse. The problem with stats, of course, is that they are faceless and voiceless, and easy to dismiss.

To cover all the aspects of abuse is better left to the many excellent books on abuse. My hope, though, is that the following story will broaden our awareness of the problem of abuse, move us past some common misunderstandings and misconceptions, motivate us to action, and most of all, give a voice and face to those who suffer at the hand of their abusers.

Reflect on this...

Were you surprised by the statistics on abuse? Why, or why not?

Have you, or someone you know, experienced abuse?

Voices and Faces of Abuse: Tom

The Church is not exempt from or immune to abuse or its affects, even though we would like to think so. "Tom," a pastor's son, knew his father's abusive pattern well. It began with a big explosion that sometimes included physical abuse, remorse from his father, and then waiting for the next incident. The one thing Tom could count on in the meantime was constant psychological abuse from his father. I call it "psychological" abuse because the way many people understand the terms "emotional" or "verbal" abuse often doesn't fully capture the weight of the devastating nonphysical blows abusers dish out to crush their victims. "Verbal abuse sounds like somebody yelled. Emotional abuse sounds like somebody cried."[4] Psychological abuse is more than someone getting their feelings hurt. It is more than yelling or angry words. Those kinds of interactions happen in any relationship. Psychological abuse, on the other hand, is an ongoing campaign used by abusers to shut their victims down and control them. Psychological abuse is an "intentional, deliberate attempt to cause mental suffering. The abuser's motivation is to achieve control now and in the future."[5]

Tom's father dealt out psychological abuse in the form of unending belittling comments, intimidation, control tactics, and condemnation. Because abusers often consider themselves superior to everyone else, they feel entitled to do and say whatever they want, no matter how hurtful or demeaning it is.

Anything Is a Reason for Abuse for the Abuser

The abuser has to stay in control, so victims of abuse will never get it right. Abusers create an environment where anything and everything can be a reason for abuse. Tom's dilemma was trying to figure out what triggered the explosive incidents in the cycle of abuse. "If I was nice, he [his dad] could go off. If I was bad, he could go off. I never knew what would set him off."

Abusers create an environment where anything and everything can be a reason for abuse.

Exhausted and frustrated by not being able to figure out what would set his dad off, Tom finally dealt with it by totally withdrawing at home, school, and from everyone. He thought that if he could become invisible by withdrawing, he could at least protect himself from the full brunt of his father's psychological punches. Unfortunately, withdrawing developed into a pattern that has affected the rest of his life and relationships.

Keep It "In House"

Tom's situation got physically abusive too. His dad used psychological abuse to tear down, belittle and crush his family. He used physical abuse to intimidate and control his family even more, proving that he was capable of following through with his threats every time he got violent. The same man who preached a trial sermon at a possible new church assignment had gotten into a fistfight with his son over a short sleeve blue shirt a few hours before. Worst of all, this abusive, hateful man that Tom knew had to be kept a secret at all costs. "It was expected of us to not talk about what happened in the home outside of the home. We were to keep everything in house." This fits the profile of an abuser perfectly.

Abusers seek to maintain a strong public image. He or she may be seen as a devoted family person or as a giving, respected church leader or as an upstanding businessperson, but behind closed doors he or she is a monster. If this person's family tries to reach out for help or tries to undermine his or her perfect image, the abuser adeptly silences and isolates them. They have had to pretend everything is fine for so long that no one believes them, they get brushed off, or people downplay the incidents. In Tom's case, when a church started to notice his dad's controlling and abusive behavior, he would just move his family to another church.

Reflect on this...

How do you feel after reading the story of Tom?

Do you think there are many people like Tom in our churches?

Being the Church for the Sufferers of Abuse

Being the Church for sufferers of abuse isn't going to be easy. I say "going to be" largely because the Church has failed to respond faithfully to sufferers of abuse. The Church has often pretended that abuse isn't an in-house problem or has ignored the issue, because it seems far too messy or big to solve or even to make a sizable dent in. Unfortunately, by pretending and ignoring, we are playing right into the hand of abusers, and allow them to tighten their grip of control. Responding faithfully will include educating ourselves about the warning signs and dynamics of abusive relationships, learning how to communicate and listen to victims of abuse, compiling and understanding the resources that offer help to sufferers of abuse (counseling, legal and law enforcement, shelters, support groups, medical), and fostering a deep, authentic compassion and care for the abused.

It may sound simple, but it isn't. Accepting people where they are in their journey is essential, because without true acceptance, steps toward healing are impossible. Unknowingly perhaps, those who don't accept or push away abused and broken people are acting like an abuser by pushing them toward isolation. That is a lonely and painful place to be.

I encourage you to read much more than just this chapter. You can learn about taking action, remaining involved, dealing with the police, safety planning, coping with harassment, legal actions, and the many other aspects and dynamics of abusive relationships.

A Word to Pastors and the Church Community

Sufferers of abuse will come to you for help, and how you respond can and will make a world of difference, either positively or negatively. Below are some guidelines that I encourage you to use and to look further into.

- Remember that talking about and reaching out for help with an abusive situation takes mounds of courage. What they fear from you the most is rejection.
- Remember abusers are masters of masking and manipulation. Don't dismiss the claims of abuse just because the person seems to be an unlikely candidate to be an abuser.
- Read the stories of sufferers of abuse to learn more about them and about the profiles of abusers.
- Be careful not to make spousal abuse a marriage problem. Saving the marriage isn't your first priority. Instead it should be helping, protecting, and planning (this is an extensive process—learn more) to help the victim of abuse. We want to honor marriage, and we should protect it but not at the expense of the victim.

- If you feel unqualified to help, make sure you connect the sufferer of abuse with counselors that understand the dynamics of abusive relationships. Call local shelters and abuse prevention organizations for the appropriate resources.
- Learn what to look for.
- Know your responsibility when it comes to reporting abuse.
- Avoid blaming the victim for the abuse. Remember abuse is always the choice of the abuser.
- Avoid minimizing the incidents of abuse but don't overreact.
- Be patient. In domestic violence situations, sufferers of abuse return to their abusers an average of five times before they leave for good.[6]

Reflect on this...

Has your understanding of abuse changed after reading this chapter? If so, how?

How would you respond to someone who confessed to you about being a victim of abuse?

Take time this week to do some reading and research on the subject of abuse.

NOTES:

6

Don't Get Hooked!

Addiction

In our culture, we have many "acceptable addictions. These addictions run rampant in our society. People can be addicted to money, material possessions, power, or even getting attention from others. All of these so-called addictions are not only common but easy to spot. The problem does not come with eating or with the accumulation of money or power but with the loss of ability to prioritize where those subjects should be placed in our everyday life. It could be argued that acceptable addictions are the fuel that drives our society. The next few pages will address some addictions that are acceptable in our society. Some of these addictions are obvious, but some are a bit more subtle.

Reflect on this...

What are all the things that can become an addiction in a person's life?

How can addictions affect our life?

A God Named Appetite

Think about it. We eat to celebrate birthdays or successes, to mourn after funerals, and every now and then for nutritional reasons. Eating food, or even eating for pleasure, is not a problem by itself. Eating can become a problem when we lose self-control. When we no longer possess the ability to choose when, where, why, and how much we eat, a culturally acceptable addiction may be taking hold. The Bible encourages us to live in such a way that demonstrates self-control. Philippians 3:19 tells us about the fate of those whose appetite is their true god. The verse says, "Their destiny is destruction, their god is their stomach, and their glory is in their shame." Certainly it is not only a physical appetite that this verse is talking about, but controlling our physical appetites is a great place to start. This is especially true in our culture, because so many of us are literally killing ourselves slowly with our daily diet. Living a life dominated by the desire to satisfy the taste buds is a poor way to structure our priorities. Controlling the appetite is also a great way to care for the temple that God has given each and every one of us, our body.

The Bible encourages us to live in such a way that demonstrates self-control.

Reflect on this...

Do you know someone who is addicted to food? If so, how does this affect his or her life?

What are some of the difficulties with maintaining a healthy eating lifestyle?

What are the ways we are to treat our bodies as temples?

Feel the Power

Power is also an acceptable addiction in our culture. People with power are respected. People with power get what they want. Powerful people can affect the fates of others by their decisions and desires. Power can be used to bring positive change, or it can selfishly bring negative change. We look up to those in power and wish that we could be like them. Sometimes, however, power can be used to coerce others to do our will instead of making their own choices.

Power is often accompanied by other desirable benefits, such as money, stability, and the respect of others. There are many wonderful things about acquiring power, but power is also something that can tempt many to focus on themselves instead of God. It is an admirable trait in our culture to be someone who is a self-made success. Think about some of the sayings we have like: "he pulled himself up by his bootstraps" or "she did it all on her own." These sayings are actually a matter of perspective, because who really does anything all by themselves? Rarely are we truly alone or on an island, yet we focus on and praise the power that we attain individually. Power becomes a means by which we do what we want.

Our motives are the key to exhibiting self-control in the power we wield in life. History is littered with those who let power consume them. Eventually those individuals paid the price, or worse, others paid it for them. Power is best used when it is used to advance the kingdom of God in legitimate ways. Power, or even a desire for power, is not a problem. Power can become an acceptable addiction when we seek it for the wrong reasons. Those living in a way that is pleasing to the Lord will seek power when it would give them the ability to help others and further the kingdom of God.

Possession Envy

Let me make it clear that there is nothing wrong with possessions. It is wrong, however, when any possession alters the way that we prioritize or approach our future. Our whole society runs on envying that next big possession that will make life more fulfilling. Envy over material possessions is an acceptable addiction in our culture.

Possessions are wonderful to have, but in the end they are not what matters in life. However, we must realize that possessions can be a blessing that we use or a master that we serve. Jesus says in Luke 12:15, "Watch out! Be on your guard against all kinds of greed; a man's life does not consist in the abundance of his possessions." In fact, when we base our life on possessions, we usually end up satisfying someone else's greed instead of our own. We end up paying the price by becoming enslaved to possessions while someone else reaps the profit. It is acceptable in our culture to be addicted to possessions, but it is not the godly way to live.

Reflect on this...

Do you know someone who is addicted to power? If so, how does this affect his or her life?

Think about your possessions. Do any of them control you in some way?

A Good Steward

In his sermon titled "The Good Steward," John Wesley accounts for three areas in life that God requires us to be good stewards.[1] He says that first, we are entrusted with our soul. Wesley goes on to explain that our soul is made in the image of God, therefore we are to use this gift in a way that glorifies God. One way that we can do this is by loving others and doing the best for them in a way that does not lord our power over them.

Second, Wesley states that God has gifted us with our bodies. Wesley goes as far as to say that our bodies are "exquisitely wrought machines." Just the thought of my body being exquisitely wrought reminds me of Psalm 139:14 which states, "I praise you because I am fearfully and wonderfully made; your works are wonderful, I know that full well." Even if we do not think our bodies are as exquisite as we would like, or even as they once were, our bodies are the temples of God and should be treated as such.

The third area that Wesley tells us God requires good stewardship is in our worldly possessions. It is good to have such possessions, but it is a problem when we are addicted to those possessions. When those possessions cause us to envy the possessions of others or begin to dominate our mind in such a way that our life is lived out for the purpose of acquiring those possessions, we are addicted to something completely acceptable to our culture. But it is not acceptable to God. God has gifted us with what we have so that we may use it to glorify Him. If we have just enough to survive, give glory to God that He is providing. If we have worldly possessions in excess, glory to God that we may be a blessing to others. We may do what we please with those possessions as long as it is not selfish or immoral in the eyes of God.

Using our power, bodies, and possessions to the glory of God is the best way to live a life of freedom. Even if addictions are acceptable, they still enslave those who are addicted to them. The yoke of overeating is unhealthy. The yoke of overpowering others will take too much from our relationships, and the yoke of being addicted to possessions will cost far more than ever imagined. In Matthew 11:30 Jesus says, “For my yoke is easy and my burden is light.” Take that easy yoke and be freed from the acceptable addictions of our culture. God will give you that freedom. Go and live in His blessing!

Reflect on this...

What does being a good steward mean to you?

What is one way this week you can be a better steward of your soul, body, and worldly possessions?

NOTES:

7

Is God a Democrat or a Republican?

Politics

Picture this scenario in your mind. It is Thanksgiving time, and you have traveled hundreds of miles to your hometown. All of your immediate and extended family has gathered together for this special holiday. Aunts, uncles, brothers, sisters, in-laws, cousins, and mom and dad are all sitting or standing in the living room enjoying each others' company. You find yourself talking with your cousin about sports, jobs, and life in general. The topic moves to economics and the state of the country. Your cousin shakes his head and says, "If my political party were in control of the country, we wouldn't be in such a mess." You feel your blood rise and without thinking you retort back, "You have got to be kidding. It was your political party's president who got us in the mess in the first place. The current president (from your political party) is just trying to dig us out!" At this point, you are both red-faced and looking a bit angry. Your uncle has overheard this conversation and decides to step in and change the subject to the weather in order to avoid an argument before turkey time. Whew! Another political debate/argument avoided.

There is an old saying that goes, "There are two things that you should never talk about . . . politics and religion." There is a bit of truth in that statement. Bringing these two subjects up always has the potential for fireworks. However, in reality, you cannot avoid them. Both profoundly affect our everyday lives.

Reflect on this...

Why do you think talking about politics and religion can lead to heated discussions with others?

What are your personal beliefs regarding the separation of church and state?

Christians and Politics

Should Christians care about politics? That is, should Christian hold public office, vote, and express their opinions openly about political issues? If so, what about the separation of church and state? Mark Noll says that "no one in the early United States took this separation of church and state to mean the absence of religious influence on public life."[1] Yet, today many feel the Church should keep their opinions to themselves and stay within the four walls of their place of worship. However, is this really possible? Better yet, should we keep our beliefs to ourselves?

The late Charles Colson, in his book *Kingdoms in Conflict*, says Christians should be involved in politics and suggests three reasons why. *First*, as citizens of the nation or state, Christians have the same civic duties all citizens have: to serve on juries, to pay taxes, to vote, and to support candidates they think are the best. *Second*, as citizens of the kingdom of God they are to bring God's standards of righteousness and justice to bear on the kingdoms of this world. *Third*, Christians have an obligation to bring moral values into public debate.[2]

The Irish philosopher Edmund Burke said, "The only thing necessary for the triumph of evil is for good men [and women] to do nothing." As disciples of Jesus Christ, can we really keep silent about things that go against God and His Word? As Christ-followers, shouldn't we speak up and take action against injustice and immorality? Francis Schaffer says, "Those who have the responsibility as Christians, as they live under Scripture, must not only take the necessary legal and political stand, but must practice all the possible Christian alternatives simultaneously with taking stands politically and legally."[3]

There are many ways to get involved and make your voice heard. Here are only some of the ways people can effect change through action:

- **Protest.** This can be done through marches, picketing, and so on. During the 1960's many people were in involved in civil rights marches. In recent days, many have been part of demonstrations to express their views on issues they feel strongly about.
- **Running for public office**. Some people feel the way to change government policies and practices is to become part of the body that makes decisions. These people feel that being in office will give a voice to those whom they represent. There are many fine Christian men and women who serve in public office.
- **Voting**. This is probably the way most people choose to voice their opinions regarding laws and government policy. Voting for or against an issue or candidate is a way people can make their voice heard and possibly change the laws and policies that go against their beliefs.
- **Boycott.** Refusing to buy from or deal with businesses whose practices go against your personal and/or religious beliefs.

Reflect on this...

Do you agree with Charles Colson that Christians should be involved in politics? Why, or why not?

Are you part of a particular political party? If so, what are the reasons you support this party?

Is God a Democrat or Republican?

Most people align themselves politically with those who, by and large, hold the same beliefs as themselves. That is, most people support the political party that best reflects their beliefs and philosophies. Both the Democrat and Republican parties are made up of people who claim their side has the best interest of the country in mind. Each election year we see candidates from both parties claim that he or she has the best interest of the country at heart. (It is interesting that most candidates have an affiliation with a Christian Church and pronounce they have a relationship with the God of the Bible.) But does God align himself with a politial party?

Several years ago I taught a Sunday School class of adults. During the class the conversation turned to politics. I mentioned that God was neither Republican nor Democrat; by the looks of some, you would have thought I had spoken a word of heresy. Since that time I have heard people bicker back and forth about whether or not you can be a Christian and be part of a certain political party. However, is that really true? Should all Christians only belong to one particular political party? Can you be a Democrat and a Christian? Can you be a Republican and a Christian? Does God align himself with one particular party? The truth is, God is neither a Democrat nor a Republican. In order to claim that God aligns himself with one particular party would be to say that He is in favor (aligns with His Word and will) of *everything* that party believes and does. Is God for higher income tax? Does He promote a particular way to provide health care? We cannot make the mistake of thinking that God favors one political party over another. The Bible makes it clear that God shows no favoritism (see Acts 10:34-35 and Romans 2:10-11).

God is neither Democrat nor Republican.

What Does this Mean?

If God is neither Republican nor Democrat does that mean we shouldn't vote or support a particular candidate? That is up to you. However, keep in mind that voting is one way we make our voice known and affect change in our communities and country. The key is voting in a way that supports a Christian/biblical worldview and the truth of Scripture. Does the issue go against Scripture? Does the candidate's view support the truth of God's Word? Granted, there are issues we vote on which do not have spiritual implications. For example, a vote to raise taxes in order to build a highway is more than likely a matter of personal opinion. However, some issues come down to right or wrong. For example, supporting laws that prohibit racism or those that help protect the innocent. Regardless of the issue or candidate, we must vote in the light of Scripture and the leading of the Holy Spirit.

The fact is both the Democratic and Republican parties have positives and negatives within them. Each party has things that are in line with Scripture as well as those things that may not. In light of this, no one can say that God is for either party. We as Christians must understand that it is our responsibility to align ourselves with God and His truth. So where do you start? Jesus said, "*Love the Lord your God with all your heart and all your soul and with all your mind. This is the first and greatest commandment. And the second is like it: 'Love your neighbor as yourself.' All the Law and the Prophets hang on these two commandments*" (Matthew 22:37-39). Also, "*So in everything, do to others what you would have them do to you, for this sums up the Law and the Prophets*" (Matthew 7:12).

Tony Campolo says God "*stands above all political parties and calls each of them into judgment. Likewise, He calls upon us to rise above all of this, and He expects us to use the Scriptures as a touchstone to test whether the policies and practices of political parties are in harmony with His will.*"[4] The question is not whether God is Republican or Democrat, but whether you are being guided by God's truth and leading, and not by a particular political party.

Reflect on this...

How does knowing God shows no favoritism help us in our relationships?

After reading this chapter, what are your thoughts about God and politics? Have your thoughts changed after reading this chapter?

NOTES:

Notes

Chapter 2

1 Hayim Hahman Bialik and Yehoshua Hana Ravnitsky, eds., *The Book of Legends* (New York: Shocken Books, 1992), 601.

2 R. T. France, *The Gospel of Matthew* (Leicester, Eng.: InterVarsity Press, 1985), 286.

Chapter 3

1 Beckford also naively ordered that, after he died, his body be placed in granite with a surrounding moat, so "no worms could get to him."

2 *New Times,* May 28—June 3, 1986, Glynn Ross (Artistic Director, Arizona Opera Company).

3 Paraphrased from an editorial in *Christianity Today.*

Chapter 5

1 Elaine Weiss, *Family and Friends' Guide to Domestic Violence: How to Listen, Talk, and Take Action When Someone You Care About Is Being Abused* (Volcano, Calif.: Volcano Press, 2003), 89.

2 http://www.now.org/issues/violence/stats.html Accessed September 25, 2012.

3 L. Bancroft, *Why Does He DO That? Inside the Minds of Angry and Controlling Men* (New York: G. P. Putnam's Sons, 2002), 22.

4 Weiss, *Family and Friends' Guide,* 38.

5 Weiss, 37-44.

6 Weiss, *Family and Friends' Guide,* 125.

Chapter 6

1 John Wesley, *Wesley's Standard Sermons,* vol. II, consisting of 44 discourses, published in four volumes in 1746, 1748, 1750, and 1760 (fourth edition 1787); to which are added 9 additional sermons, published in Vols. I to IV of Wesley's collected works, 1771/edited and annotated by Edward H. Sugden (London: Epworth Press, 1921), 463-67.

Chapter 7

1 Knoll, Mark. *A History of Christianity in the United States and Canada* (Grand Rapids: Wm. B. Eerdman's Co., 1992), p. 83.

2 Miller, Stephen M., ed. *Christians at Work in a Hurting World* (Kansas City: Beacon Hill Press of Kansas City, 1990), p. 13.

3 Schaeffer, Francis. *A Christian Manifesto* (Westchester: Crossway Books, 1981, p. 132-133.

4 Campolo, Tony. *Is Jesus A Republican or a Democrat?* (Dallas: Word Publishing, Co., 1995), p. 3.

Further Reading

Dan Boone. *A Charitable Discourse: Talking About Things that Divide Us* (Beacon Hill Press of Kansas City)

Barbara Curtis. *Reaching the Right From the Left: Talking About Social Issues with People Who Don't Think Like You* (Beacon Hill Press of Kansas City)

Paul Hegstrom. *Broken Children, Grown-Up Pain* (Revised): *Understanding the Effects of Your Wounded Past* (Beacon Hill Press of Kansas City)

Brett Rickey. *Chasing Cool: Examining the Pursuits of Your Heart* (Beacon Hill Press of Kansas City)

Other Dialog studies also available!

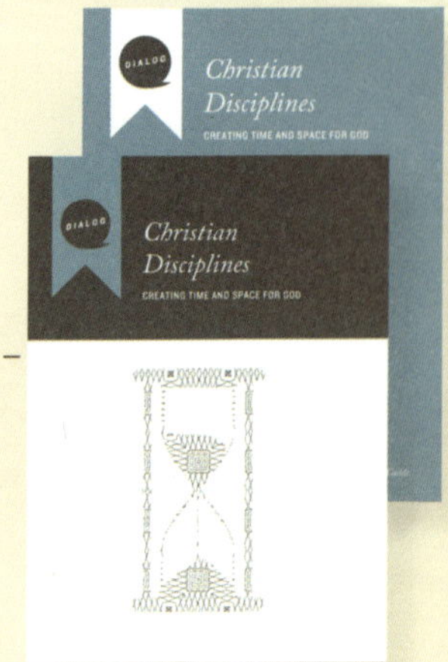

CHRISTIAN DISCIPLINES
Creating Time and Space for God

Disciplines that contribute to the transformation of our hearts and lives enable us to increase our capacity to love God and others. See how *reading, praying, connecting, fasting, giving,* and *receiving* are important practices to integrate into your daily walk with God.

PARTICIPANT'S GUIDE ISBN: 978-0-8341-2980-1
FACILITATOR'S GUIDE ISBN: 978-0-8341-2986-3

TAKE UP YOUR MAT
And Other Miracles from the Gospel of John

The miracles Jesus performed had a definite impact on the lives of those who experienced them and contain a powerful message for those of us living today. *Take Up Your Mat* unpacks seven miracles found in the gospel of John and explores their message in our current context.

PARTICIPANT'S GUIDE ISBN: 978-0-8341-2981-8
FACILITATOR'S GUIDE ISBN: 978-0-8341-2987-0

Available online at DialogSeries.com